THE
MEETINGS POCKETBOOK

By Patrick Forsyth
Drawings by Phil Hailstone

"A wealth of succinct and sensible advice. Don't arrange or attend another meeting without reading it!"
Gill Smillie, Chief Executive, Conference Venues Countrywide (and a founder member of the Meetings Industry Association).

"A complete guide showing how to make meetings more effective, as a chairperson or participant. It may be common sense but we can all benefit from this straightforward reminder of the rules."
Pippa Bourne, Head of Non-accredited Programmes, Institute of Management.

THE AGENDA

INTRODUCTION

'The ideal meeting is two; with one absent'

MEETINGS (BLOODY?) MEETINGS

'That last meeting was just great.' How often do you say that?
How often are the meetings you attend (or conduct) *really* constructive and useful?
How quickly do they help you reach decisions or action?
Do they always turn out as you wish? Always?
Meetings of whatever sort (long/short; formal/informal) can be...

- Ineffective
- Divisive
- Interminably boring

...and infuriating, hard work, tedious and – at worst – a complete waste of time.

Yet, they should be useful; and can be too. The first thing to be said about meetings is that successful ones do not just happen. You need to work at them; *everybody* needs to work at them.

The first question: what exactly is a meeting?

INTRODUCTION

FIRST, WHAT IS A MEETING?

This may seem an obvious question. It is a group of people, gathered together to discuss, debate or decide. And it can cause problems.

Every meeting must be planned, considered and conducted with an eye on how it can be made to go well; the alternative can all too easily be chaos.

So, whether the meeting is...

- Large or small
- Formal or informal
- Long or short

...and whatever the seniority, level of experience, roles and intentions of those present, it must be well run – with attention to detail – if it is to have a real chance of being successful.

But beware. Do not think only formal meetings need care and attention – they all do, even two people spending 10 minutes together. It is often the less apparently formal meetings where neglect can all too easily allow problems to occur.

WHAT MEETINGS CAN DO

Meetings are simply a form of communication, and can be useful to...

- Inform
- Analyse or solve problems
- Discuss and exchange views
- Inspire or motivate
- Counsel or reconcile conflict
- Obtain opinion or feedback
- Persuade

- Train or develop
- Reinforce the status quo
- Instigate change in knowledge, skills or attitude

...and must often achieve several of these during one meeting.

Overall, the object is often to prompt decision, action or change – all with constructive goals in mind.

INTRODUCTION

THE COST OF MEETINGS

Meetings can be costly. They may need a venue, equipment (visual aids), refreshments –
but, above all – they require **time**:

- **Time** for preparation
- **Time** for getting there
- **Time** for attending

What is more, all this time is multiplied by the number of people involved. A two hour
meeting of eight people demands sixteen hours, which could be twenty or more if you
include preparation or travel.

What does all this cost? As an example, someone on a salary of £35,000 per year will
(once pension, package and other costs are included) cost at least £30 per hour. In the
example above, if everyone present is on that salary the cost is over £500! And that is
just the people.

The potential value of any meeting must be weighed against the costs.

THE OPPORTUNITY COST

You must also bear in mind the opportunity cost. In other words, think about what else could be going on if people were not in a meeting, and how much those other activities would be worth.

Again, multiply by the number of people. If they were all doing something else, what would be achieved and **would that be more worthwhile than the meeting?**

So never:

- Say, 'it is *just* a meeting'
- Assume the cost is negligible
- Fail to consider all the costs

Think in terms of meeting 'man-hours' and make sure they will be worthwhile.

If a meeting is necessary, so be it, but (and it is a big but) it still has to be made productive.

THE DANGERS

While meetings can, indeed must, be constructive and useful, it is worth having the dangers in mind in order actively to avoid them.

Here are nine examples of what a bad meeting can do…

- Waste time
- Waste money
- Divert attention from more important tasks
- Slow down progress and delay action
- Be divisive
- Lower morale
- Be a platform for the talkative and disruptive
- Breed office politics
- Create muddle or chaos

…and end up making few (or bad) decisions; or in tears.

DESPITE THE DANGERS...

Though bad meetings can be a disaster, good meetings are not only useful in specific, practical ways – but also, *people want them*.

Having too few meetings can be as much a mistake as having too many. For most people, meetings have a number of merits (and these may be separate from the business reasons for the meeting). For example, meetings:

- Keep people informed and up-to-date
- Create involvement with others
- Provide a chance to be heard
- Are social gatherings
- Allow contact with people in different parts/functions within the organisation
- Can involve useful informal communication before and after the formal business
- Provide visibility and an opportunity for personal public relations
- Can broaden experience and act as a learning opportunity

Remember, people are quick to complain about meetings, but this may only mean those they attend are badly run or irrelevant to them. *Good* meetings can be useful in their own right – and improve morale.

BEFORE THE MEETING

THE BIG QUESTION

Given the cost and the difficulty of ensuring successful and worthwhile meetings, the first question that should be asked when scheduling one is simple:
Is the meeting really necessary?

Let us be blunt: the problem with some meetings is not that they are badly organised, last too long or come to no real conclusion, *it is that they never should have been held in the first place*.

- Do not hold meetings for the wrong reason (or for no reason at all)

- Think of the time and cost involved

- **Make preparation a priority**

A MEETING OR...?

Before you open your mouth to say, 'Let's set a meeting', **consider the alternatives**.

Never call a meeting without asking:

- Is it a matter for debate or consultation?
- Can information be circulated in any other way?
- Can you telephone, write a memo/e-mail, or issue an instruction?

Can you, in fact, do *anything* else?

Remember that what is easiest for you, namely sitting everyone round the table and telling them something, may not be time-efficient for others or the best way of achieving results. A meeting can very easily make a mountain out of a molehill. On some matters, a word in the corridor or a chat over lunch may be an adequate exchange.

Perhaps the moral here is the same as that sometimes given to those contemplating matrimony: **if in doubt, don't!**

BEFORE THE MEETING

WHO SHOULD ATTEND?

This is a key question as is, 'Who should *not* attend?'. Remember, as a rule of thumb, the more people present the longer it will all take.

Think about...

- Who must be there
- Who should be an observer
- Who might find it useful
- Who has an axe to grind

- Who has something positive to contribute
- Who will make unnecessary problems or otherwise dilute effectiveness

...and **assemble the right group in a considered manner, matching:**

- Expertise to the topic to be discussed
- Authority to the decisions that must be made

Everyone must have a clear reason for their presence.

14

WHO DOES WHAT?

A meeting may need a range of different people attending it – people from different departments and functions, and with different expertise. It will also need:

- A chairperson (see *Leading the Meeting*); *whatever* the nature and size of the meeting someone must direct it

- A secretary, either to officiate procedure, or to take minutes. The minute taker can simply be one of the participants. If so it may need to be someone with a minor role so that their attention is not overstretched across both their contribution and the need to make notes

Some meetings will need others with special 'meetings roles' – to organise the visual aids, the paperwork or the refreshments.

There are key tasks and decisions that must be attended to **before the meeting takes place**. So, for example, the chair should be nominated before the meeting as that is when his/her responsibilities begin.

Decide on key roles and players ahead of the meeting.

BEFORE THE MEETING

BE SELECTIVE

1. Who should attend your meetings?

In selecting, beware of using the wrong criteria. The emphasis should be on the business of the meeting itself (though other reasons, eg training, may be important) and not so much on:

- Company politics
- Who you owe a favour to (which might mean they are asked to attend; or not!)
- Democracy
- Social factors

2. Which meetings should you attend?

If you are asked to attend someone else's meeting: **think first before you accept**.

Some meetings are unavoidable, but you have probably sat through many and thought, 'Why am I wasting my time on this?'.

Most of us have plenty to do rather than sit in a meeting. If the meeting is necessary, perhaps the presence of some is not.

A REASON FOR MEETING

Meetings are held every day without real – or clear – **objectives**, and take longer and fail to be effective as a result. Objectives must be *specific*. Do *not* meet to:

- Start the planning process
- Discuss cost savings
- Review training needs
- Streamline administration

Set **clear, detailed objectives**. For example: 'to decide how to reduce the advertising budget by 10 per cent over the next six months' is a better objective than simply, 'to discuss reducing expenditure'. Clearly defined and realistic objectives make for a clear outcome.

Objectives set the scene for an effective meeting.

A REASON FOR MEETING
HOW IT HELPS

Having a specific reason, and clear objectives, for a meeting will have a number of effects...

- People will be clear *why* the meeting is being held
- They will be better able, and perhaps more inclined, to prepare
- The discussion should be better focused
- Discussion will be easier to control

...and the meeting is more likely to achieve its desired result.

Consider also whether it will help to have a note of the objectives in writing, and perhaps circulated to the participants in advance.

If you ever attend meetings where the objectives are unclear, **ask what they are** and take a moment to clarify them. The meeting that follows will always go better.

AN EFFECTIVE FOUNDATION

The word *agenda* comes from Latin and literally means, 'those things which must be done'.

This is basic, but probably goes further than anything else to ensure a successful meeting (especially in conjunction with clear objectives).

So:

ALWAYS have a clear agenda

(this applies *however* large or small, formal or informal the meeting)

Ideally, the agenda should be in **writing** and **circulated in advance** to those attending; otherwise the meeting may well grind to a halt in confusion, wasting time and effort and achieving nothing.

BEFORE THE MEETING

HOW AN AGENDA HELPS

An agenda must reflect the objectives and:

- Order the items for discussion and review
- Pick up and link to points from any previous meetings, to ensure continuity
- Provide opportunity (as it is compiled) for people to input to the meeting content
- Specify who will lead or contribute to each item (in part to facilitate preparation)
- Reflect any 'hidden' agenda (placing controversial items appropriately)
- Deal with administrative matters (eg time and location)
- Specify the formalities (the need for a secretary, for visual aids to be prepared etc)

The agenda must balance the meeting. It will allow controlled discussion and facilitate successful completion of the business in hand.

CONSIDER THE REALITIES

Whether you plan a long formal meeting or a brief, 'Can you spare me 10 minutes?', you have to be realistic when setting the agenda. Ask:

- Can my list of items be dealt with in an hour or 10 minutes, or is something more extensive (including more than one meeting) necessary?
- Is there sufficient lead time to give notice, for people to prepare etc?
- Will one major, or contentious, item overpower all else, either taking too long or taking minds off other lesser items?
- Is the combination of items for discussion/decision and those attending right? (eg you cannot make decisions on expenditure if the budget-holders aren't present)
- Is the planned style of meeting compatible with intentions? (eg teaching/training takes more time than giving out information)

It is too late once a meeting is under way to discover 'organisational gaps', and the credibility of the whole thing may be threatened by one significant practical oversight.

BEFORE THE MEETING

DECIDING THE SEQUENCE

Two points are important here:

- Selecting an appropriate order does make a difference to the resulting meeting
- There are no clear rules as to what works best

Is an item:

- Appropriate early on, to get it out of the way/while we are fresh?
- Easier linked logically to other items (horses first, carts second)?
- Most dependent on preparation?
- Interesting/important to everyone attending or just a few?
- In danger of taking up too much time and overshadowing other items?

Also bear in mind what may be awkward, unpopular, contentious or easy, straightforward and quick.

TIMING

Timing is the key to a successful meeting.

Meetings can go wrong in many ways as a result of poor timing, eg:

- Too short, and half the agenda has to be carried over
- Too long, going round the houses and adding nothing by extending the time
- Unbalanced, spending too long in some areas, skimping others

The timing of a meeting and its agenda must be planned and organised practically to help the meeting go well.

BEFORE THE MEETING

WHEN TO HOLD IT

The likely duration of the meeting will dictate when in the day it can be held which, in turn, can influence its effectiveness.

For example:

	Positive	**Negative**
9.00 am	Avoids telephone interruptions. Leaves the rest of the day clear	Latecomers (travel problems) will cause disruption
Before lunch 11 am	Lunch provides a natural finishing point	Productivity drops dramatically as people get hungry
Late afternoon 3.30 pm +	Easier to keep to time (people want to go home)	Tiredness and lack of concentration late in the day

So, consider not just when meetings are scheduled to fit the diary, but **that timing can affect the sort of meeting that it will be**.

TIME-EFFECTIVE

Meetings should always be time-effective. This means they should:

- Be no longer than necessary to achieve their ends
- Have no more people than is necessary

Every corner of the day should be considered if it will make good use of the time.

If that means certain key meetings happen out of hours – in the evening, at weekends, on a journey, over a meal – then so be it. Provided this does not get out of hand, and meetings are considered constructively whenever and wherever they take place, it can be a useful approach.

A START *AND* A FINISH

As well as a start time, every meeting **should also have a finishing time**. In most organisations people are just too busy to attend a meeting with no idea whether it will last half an hour or all morning; it encourages attention to wander as people worry about later commitments. A stated intention to finish at a specific time will:

- Act as a courtesy to people, perhaps gaining more commitment to the meeting as a result

- Help keep the meeting on track: half-way through the time, it should be half-way through the content

- Appear more professional, and help set the discipline all meetings need

Having a clear duration in mind for the meeting makes it easier to control and more likely to be successful.

TIMING THE CONTENT

To give a real chance of sticking to a planned duration, consider **having a timed agenda**.

For example, allocate a proposed time for each item, certainly for main sections and topics. This will act to focus discussion and give both chairperson and participants something to aim at.

Even being able to say, 'Let's try to get this item out of the way in the next 20 minutes', will be of psychological value in concentrating minds. It really helps.

Ensure that the meeting has a timed structure, publish it, refer to it as the meeting proceeds, and aim to stick to it as far as possible.

PHYSICAL ENVIRONMENT

The room and location for a meeting and the equipment available also make a difference.

The hazards are many:

- Too many people in too small a smoke-filled room and everyone is uncomfortable, concentration goes out of the window (though the smoke never seems to do so!)
- Uncomfortable chairs also affect concentration
- No visual aid equipment available can double the time needed to explain, say, diagrams
- Inappropriate refreshment arrangements create interruptions

And so on and so on; think of meetings you have attended.

The moral: meetings need to be held...

- In the right place
- In the right room
- With the right equipment

...all arranged in advance.

BEFORE THE MEETING

WHERE TO HOLD IT: *IN?*

Sometimes important meetings will need arranging away from the office (see next page). However, most need to be in the office and in a suitable room, which is:

- Quiet
- Private, if necessary (this may mean soundproof)
- Of sufficient size
- Comfortable (chairs, table and other furniture well designed)
- Air-conditioned, if necessary, especially if you plan to allow smoking (still a vexed issue, but the majority are now non-smokers and increasingly the norm is not to allow it in meetings)
- Right in terms of ambience, neither too plush nor too spartan
- Of a layout that allows good visibility (of people and visual aids); acoustics too need considering
- Equipped with power points, good lighting, but *no* telephone

Do not just say, 'Let's have it in George's office'. **Think about what room will be best and plan accordingly.**

WHERE TO HOLD IT: *OUT?*

For more serious, and longer, meetings the first decision is: in or out?

Some meetings warrant the time and cost of leaving the office and its distractions behind. For example, a senior planning meeting may be difficult to fit in, but vital; two days away – perhaps residentially (maybe over a weekend) – could complete something that might otherwise take weeks.

If this is advisable, a good venue can pay back its cost in terms of results very easily. It can be motivational too. Any external venue should be carefully chosen regarding: location, cost, facilities, atmosphere, privacy and ability to cope with special requirements (eg visual aids).

The results wanted should be the guide here (and the fact that some meetings are best away from the office should not become an excuse for making every one a 'jolly').

BASIC EQUIPMENT AND FACILITIES

Having the right equipment prevents distractions and delay and helps everything go smoothly. Consider whether you need...

- Pens/pencils
- Water and glasses
- Namecards

- Ashtrays (or *not*)
- Coffee on standby
- Overhead projector/other visual aids

...and, for larger or more formal meetings:

- Lectern
- Microphone

**Have a meetings
checklist of such
things and meetings
will never be disrupted
by someone saying,
'Sorry, do you
have a pencil?'.**

BEFORE THE MEETING

VISUAL AIDS

Without a doubt visual aids help most meetings.
They…

- Aid understanding
- Illustrate
- Focus attention
- Vary the pace

…and *exemplify* the message someone is aiming to put over.

They can take many forms, from a simple handout that all present can have in front of them to computer generated slides.

IS THIS CLEAR NOW?

Three rules for visual aids:

- **Have some** (they really do make a difference)
- **Prepare them carefully** (ensure they are legible and clear)
- **Check (and double-check) any equipment they use** (there is nothing worse than announcing the way in which a graph will make clear the complex figures and ratios involved and then finding a fuse has gone)

VISUAL AIDS

WHAT YOU MIGHT USE

- **Flipcharts**: simple, require no electricity and can display prepared material or be used as a 'workpad' as you go
- **Overhead projectors**: can be used seated. Can show prepared slides. Take written notes on sheets or roll of acetate. Allow material to be masked and displayed progressively. But they need a little practice to handle effectively
- **Tabletop presenters**: all the advantages of the flipchart but portable, though only large enough to use with a smaller group
- **Whiteboards**: have replaced the old blackboard and are a good 'workpad'. Unlike flipcharts you cannot turn over and refer back, and *you must remember to use the right pens or they will not clean off at all!*
- **Handouts**: perhaps the easiest of all, combining the ability to circulate in advance with visualisation. Everybody can look at them together

Choice will depend on the nature and size of the meeting and what the participants are familiar and comfortable with.

VISUAL AIDS

DEATH BY POWERPOINT

We have all sat through seemingly endless sequences of PowerPoint slides. Of course, these are useful and convenient (thank you Microsoft) but there are hazards too. Do not:

- Overdo the number of slides
- Pack too much information onto each slide
- Turn pages from documents into slides without reconfiguring them (a prime cause of over-full slides)
- Add meaningless pictures, the relevance of which is unclear
- Leave a slide projecting long after you have finished referring to it (press the 'B' key on the computer and it will blank the screen)

These errors result from technology driving the action; always think of what a slide should do in context.

VISUAL AIDS

MAKING THE BEST USE OF THEM

The basic rules are:

- Keep the content simple
- Restrict the number of words
- Use diagrams, graphs and illustrations wherever possible (and never try to deal with figures without visual support)
- Keep them fresh (use colour and design to make them interesting)
- Let them reflect the agenda
- Make sure that what the visuals show matches what is said
- Make them relevant (so they demand to be seen)
- Make sure they are visible/legible
- Do not let them distract (remove them once the point is made)
- Tell people when copies will/will not be available (to avoid unnecessary copying)

There is truth in the old saying that a picture is worth a thousand words.

THE MEETING BEFORE THE MEETING

One of the most important truths about meetings is that much of the business is, in fact, completed *before* the meeting even takes place.

In other words, it is the informal gatherings – of two here, three there, debating what they want to happen and **planning joint strategies** to act in accord on the day – that are a major influence on what transpires at the actual meeting.

This means you should:

- Never underestimate this factor or assume others will not use it
- Take time to form any necessary alliances
- Watch for signs of other such alliances, anticipate their effect on the meeting and plan accordingly
- Bear in mind that both invisible and visible alliances can be useful (though it may be wise to assume people know you are having such discussions)

Overall, use the informal communications networks, and the grapevine, as an active part of preparing for a meeting.

BEFORE THE MEETING

NOT STARTING ON TIME

Imagine ..... the meeting is set for 10am. People start to congregate, the appointed time arrives but not everyone has appeared. It is decided to 'give them five minutes', coffee is poured, various ad hoc (and probably not very useful) discussions start amongst different groups. Time passes and finally the meeting starts fifteen minutes late with one person still to arrive. Just as the meeting is getting down to business, the latecomer turns up, apologies and recapping waste another five minutes, and the meeting starts again. You probably know the scene.

If there are, say, eight people involved in the situation described it is easy to waste eight times half an hour – that is, four man-hours and without, in some organisations, it even appearing unusual!

Starting meetings late wastes time (disproportionately), can be resented by many who are punctual and thus causes friction instead of starting on a positive note.

STARTING ON TIME

This is worth emphasis:

Always start meetings on time.

It may be awkward to start with, but it is the only way to instil good habits and respect for time. If you are new to a company or department then start as you mean to go on. Be consistent.

Let the word go round: 'You'd better not be late for George's meetings'.

It is worth the effort.

So, two rules here:
- **If you are a participant: be punctual**
- **If it is your meeting: be punctual yourself and START ON TIME**

REGULAR MEETINGS

'Why are we having this meeting?'
'Well, it's a month since the last one.'

Before any meeting becomes a regular one –
weekly or monthly, say – someone must think
long and hard. Ask:

- What frequency is *really* necessary?

- How many are required in a year? (often a monthly meeting is created when nine or ten would be better; it may not be as neat but it saves time)

- What placement of them suits? (eg more at some times of year, less at others)

Once decided it makes sense to schedule the meetings well ahead, arranging dates for, say, the next six or even for the year. This avoids the constant juggling of diaries that is necessary to get any group of people together. You can always cancel any that later prove unnecessary.

Never allow meetings to perpetuate unnecessarily.

NOTES

LEADING THE MEETING
(And handling discussion)

Tips for participants as well as those in the chair

A FIRM HAND ON THE TILLER

Every meeting needs someone in charge. This used to be the chairman but is now more often the chairperson or, less elegantly, the chair. Call them what you will, but make sure there is one. And not just anyone, an appropriate one. Their role, as we shall see, is substantial.

The benefits of a well directed meeting include:

- Better focus on objectives
- Discussion can be kept more constructive
- A thorough review can be assured before decisions are taken
- All sides of the argument can be reflected, and balanced
- Proceedings can be kept businesslike and less argumentative (even when dealing with contentious issues)

A good chairperson will lead the meeting, handle the discussion and act to see objectives are met, promptly, efficiently, effectively and without waste of time.

GET THE RIGHT LEADER

In the light of the responsibilities listed, the importance of the right choice of a suitable leader is clearly apparent.

No meeting will run smoothly without a good leader (even if this is just one of two).

Get the right person in the chair before the meeting starts and accept that someone must be in charge. Points can still be made but order prevailing will help the whole process along.

TWO KEY RULES

Whatever else the leader does or does not do, he/she must impose and stick to two key rules:

1. **Only one person should talk at any one time**
2. **The leader decides who**

Stick to these two and much else will take care of itself.

LEADER'S RESPONSIBILITIES

Leading a meeting is a major task. Chairpeople need to have their wits about them and to deploy skills that must be learned and practised. It is worth some study.

Whoever is directing a meeting must:

- Command the respect of those attending
- Do their homework and come prepared, having read any relevant documents and taken any other action necessary to help them 'take charge' (they should also encourage others to prepare, as this makes for more considered and succinct contributions to the meeting and saves time)
- Be punctual
- Start on time
- Ensure administrative matters will be taken care of correctly (eg refreshments, taking minutes etc)

LEADER'S RESPONSIBILITIES

They must:

- Start on the right note and lead into the agenda
- Introduce the people, if necessary (and certainly know who's who themselves – namecards can help at some kinds of meeting)
- Set the rules
- Control the discussion, and the individual types present (the talkative, the quiet, the argumentative etc)
- Encourage contributions where necessary
- Ask questions to clarify (this can be a great time saver). Always query something unclear at once. If the meeting runs on when something has been misinterpreted, it will take longer to sort out and you will have to recap and re-cover a section)
- Ensure everybody has their say
- Keep the discussion to the point

LEADER'S RESPONSIBILITIES

They must:

- Listen, as in LISTEN. The leader resolves any 'But you said .....' arguments
- Watch the clock and remind people of the time pressure
- Summarise, clearly and succinctly, where necessary, which usually means regularly
- Ensure decisions are actually made, agreed and recorded
- Cope with upsets, outbursts and emotion
- Provide the final word (summary) and bring matters to a conclusion (and link to any final administrative detail; things like setting another meeting date are often forgotten)
- See, afterwards, to any follow up action (another great timewaster is people arriving at meetings not having taken action promised at a previous session)
- Do all this with patience, goodwill, humour and respect for the various individuals present

GETTING OFF TO A GOOD START

It may be a cliché that **first impressions** last, but it is true – and important too. It is something which, by definition, you can only get one shot at.

Start the meeting in a way that:

- Is positive
- Makes its purpose (and procedure) clear
- Establishes your authority and right to be in charge
- Creates the right atmosphere
- Generates interest and enthusiasm for what is to come
- Is immediately perceived as businesslike

An effective start makes everything thereafter more likely to go well.

PROMPTING DISCUSSION

Meetings need to be kept short. However, it is important to get adequate and representative discussion, otherwise decisions may be taken on incomplete information.

Sometimes the necessary information is not forthcoming. There may be a variety of reasons for this…

● Fear of rejection

● Pressure of other, perhaps more senior, people

● Lack of preparation

● Incomplete understanding of the issues

…or simply a perceived lack of encouragement to contribute.

So, the rule here must be actively to encourage any inputs that are not forthcoming.

The leader must ask participants for their views and do so in a way that prompts open and considered contributions.

QUESTIONING TECHNIQUES

Questions from the chair must not lead. If the chairperson says, 'I think that is an excellent suggestion, what do you think?', it may make it difficult to disagree, especially if someone senior is in the chair.

Also consider what style of question is appropriate:

Open questions
These cannot be answered 'yes' or 'no'. They tend to start with the words, 'what, why, where, when, how, who' or with phrases such as: 'Tell us what you think about...' They are much the best at getting people to talk.

Closed questions
These tend to produce a terse chain of 'yes' and 'no' answers, eg following questions such as: 'Do you think that makes sense?'

How questions are asked affects the response. If a simple 'yes' is all that is required, a closed question will suffice, otherwise open questions should predominate.

SIX WAYS OF ASKING FOR VIEWS

1. **Overhead question** – put to the group as a whole and useful to start things off
2. **Overhead/directed** – put to the group as a whole (to get everyone thinking) and then aimed at an individual for first comment: 'Now what do we feel about this issue? David, what's your view?'
3. **Direct to one person** – to get an individual response or check understanding
4. **Rhetorical** – a question demanding no answer, but which makes a point or prompts thinking, while allowing the chairperson to provide the answer if appropriate
5. **Re-directed question** – a question asked of the chair and deflected back to the group: 'That's a fair question, what *do* we think about that?'
6. **Development question** – builds on the answer to an earlier question by moving it around the group: 'So, Sarah thinks it will be too expensive. Are there other problems?'

Prompting discussion is as important as control; without it the meeting will be unbalanced and may be less effective as a result.

ENSURE QUESTIONS ARE ANSWERED

It is one thing to ask good questions but comment may not be immediately forthcoming.

1. **Ask again** – persevere, rephrase the question (it is always possible it was not understood) and ensure that the point is clear and that people know a comment really is required

2. **Use silence** – often even a short silence after a question is awkward. So the leader moves on, perhaps to someone else.

If you really want a comment then *wait*. And make it clear that you are prepared to give the person a moment, as you are keen to have their opinion. Even a few seconds longer will usually succeed in getting a comment; it only needs a modicum of patience. Maybe the point deserves a moment's thought.

Do not miss what may be important contributions by being over hasty.

LEADING THE MEETING

CONCENTRATE ON BUSINESS IN HAND

A good meeting requires concentration. Beware interruptions! Messages ('Excuse me a moment, I *must* attend to this one'), mobile telephones, or simply the tea and coffee arriving, all delay the proceedings and take eyes off the ball.

It helps therefore if:

- Rules are laid down about messages
- Breaks are organised (for longer meetings) so that people know when they will have a moment to check their desks
- Refreshments are organised in advance
- Others outside the meeting (including switchboard operators and secretaries) are briefed as to how things will work

Finally, if there are interruptions, do not compete with them, wait until they have passed.

Make the meeting concentrate on the meeting.

ENCOURAGE CREATIVITY

Good meetings should be creative. They should:

- Stimulate thinking ('two heads are better than one')
- Generate new ideas
- Find new ways of looking at things
- Instigate change
- Consider novel solutions
- Solve problems

Yet, new ideas can prompt a negative cycle of events. The leader must be careful to get members to suspend judgment and give unfamiliar ideas a chance to be reviewed. Don't let the discussion revolve around 'scoring points', with people (effectively) saying: 'Your idea's no good, here's a better one'.

Creativity needs fostering and ideas need constructive review.

CAUSES OF CONFLICT

People's job functions and objectives often create inherent differences of view, which can lead to conflict. Here are some examples of how just a few factors can be viewed very differently by those in three key functions:

	Finance	Production	Marketing
Objective	To ensure that the return on capital employed will provide security, growth and yield	To optimise cost/output relationships	To maximise profitable sales in the marketplace
Time period of operation	Largely past: analysing results plus some forecasting	Largely present: keeping production going, particularly in 3-shift working	Largely future: because of lead time in reacting to marketplace
Orientation	Largely inward: concerned with internal results of company	Largely inward: concerned with factory facilities for personnel	Largely outward: concerned with customers, distribution and competition

CAUSES OF CONFLICT

	Finance	Production	Marketing
Attitudes to money	Largely 'debit and credit': once money spent, it is gone; money not spent is saved	Largely 'cost effective': hence value analysis techniques and cost cutting	Largely 'return on investment': money 'invested' in promotion to provide 'return' in sales and and profits
Personality	Often introverted; lengthy training; makes decisions on financially quantifiable grounds	Usually qualified in quantitative discipline; makes decisions on input/output basis	Often extroverted; often educationally unqualified; has to make some decisions totally qualitatively

Such differences are not only inherent, they are necessary if individuals are to do their own jobs well. Recognising where conflict may occur is the first step to resolving it.

(This analysis comes from Marketing for Non-Marketing Managers, Patrick Forsyth, Pitmans/IM)

PROBLEM PEOPLE

Some people, whatever their views, are essentially constructive in how they interact in a meeting. Others are, well, just downright difficult. All pose different problems and need different responses. Here are the top six:

THE TALKATIVE SHOW-OFF

Wants attention, is an enthusiast for the topic, or is trying to monopolise the conversation to demonstrate personal expertise.

Action

The first job is to get a word in. Pounce on any pause (even just a breath) and call a halt to the input, ideally with a positive comment or a word of thanks. Then move on, selecting a new starting point or throwing the ball to someone else. You can use the group – 'What do others think of that view?' – or ask a specific question: 'What John has said raises the question of costs. What do you think those are likely to be, Mary?'.

Avoid these people wasting time, and beware of not getting to the sense that may lie within their long spiel.

PROBLEM PEOPLE

THE GUSHER

The too talkative may harbour more sinister motives; they may simply be intent on drowning others out to ensure their view receives more than its fair share of time.

Action

The timed agenda and good discipline will help here. Otherwise it is again necessary to interrupt, to summarise or ask for a summary, or focus the input on just one thing: 'Before we open it up still further, will you summarise your view of just stage one, please?'. Once the ball is with the chair it can be passed specifically to another participant in the meeting.

PROBLEM PEOPLE
THE SPHINX

Almost as difficult to deal with as those who say too much, are those who remain too silent, especially when you know their input could be valuable. They may be timid, shy, bored, indifferent, inexperienced or lacking the confidence to have their say.

Action
Asking questions is the best route here. Ask an easy question to get them started and, if necessary, make comments that bolster their confidence.

If they are well able to speak but are choosing not to do so, then ask a difficult or pointed question. Alternatively, ask for their assistance: 'Anita, with your experience you must have some good advice about this. What do you think?' (and yes, a little flattery can help).

PROBLEM PEOPLE

THOSE WHO HOLD SEPARATE MEETINGS

Whispering can be constructive (a thought prompted by the discussion) or it can show a lack of understanding, bored digression or, even, plotting.

Action
Getting the meeting to pause isolates the chatter in the silence and this alone may be sufficient to stop it. A question may identify if there is a problem or if something is unclear. If so, a digression to sort it may make sense.

The rule of only one person talking at one time should be observed consistently.

PROBLEM PEOPLE
THE CHIP ON THE SHOULDER

This is the person with the pet gripe, or who feels hard done by in some respect. This may well be so, but the meeting is unlikely to be the place to sort it out. Often this person wants to lay blame on someone at the meeting.

Action
You must check whether the, perhaps unspecific, gripes conceal a real point. Ask the griper to be specific, refer back to the clear purpose of the meeting, use the group to confirm the need to concentrate. A promise to discuss some other matter later, if appropriate, may help get the distraction put on one side.

LEADING THE MEETING

PROBLEM PEOPLE
THE DEVIOUS

There are, inevitably, many reasons why
people do not say exactly what they
mean, eg concern for the longer-term
strategy or fear of losing face. The devious
person may underplay, overstate or disguise
the facts; even, sometimes, be economical
with the truth.

Action
Learn to 'read between the lines', recognising that
something beyond the basic objectives of the
meeting is going on. What to do next depends
very much on circumstances. Sometimes longer-
term or peripheral issues need to be progressed in
parallel. Sometimes deviousness must be stamped
on at once.

HANDLING DISORDER

Even in the best run organisations meetings occasionally get out of hand. What do you do?

- Never get upset or emotional yourself
- Pick on one element being expressed and try to isolate and deal with that without heat
- Agree, before regrouping ('You're quite right. This is a contentious issue, emotions are bound to run high. However, let's .....')

If disorder continues, you have a few options:

- Call for a few minutes complete silence, before attempting to restate
- Announce a short break, and insist it is taken
- Leave the item causing problems until later (though make it quite clear when and how it will be dealt with or matters may get worse)
- Abandon the meeting until another time (this is the worst option and very much to be avoided but better than prolonged disorder)

Above all (with apologies to Douglas Adams) **DON'T PANIC!**

KEEP AN EYE ON THE CLOCK

Timing, as has been mentioned before, is crucial to any meeting.

Watch the time and fine-tune everything with regard to the time remaining as the meeting proceeds. This is as important for the leader as it is for the participants.

PARTICIPATING IN THE MEETING

Tips for the leader as well as for participants

THE FIRST QUESTION

Meetings can waste time, effort and money. Yet, not having necessary meetings can result in a lack of ideas, debate, communication or decisions – which is not good either.

Every time you are invited to attend a meeting, think about...

- What you can contribute
- What you can get from it

...that you cannot get any other way. (You may be able to make an adequate input by submitting a note or just reading the minutes afterwards.) Of course, one must be realistic: some meetings come with a three-line whip, otherwise resolve:

Never to attend a meeting unless you are convinced it is genuinely useful.

HOW TO PARTICIPATE EFFECTIVELY

There is an old saying that you only get out of something what you put in, and it is certainly true of meetings. The key things that will help you make your participation effective are:

- Adequate **preparation**: you will never get value from a meeting if you do not know what is going on or are not ready to make an effective contribution
- **Looking the part**
- Making sure your **communication is effective**: this applies to what you say and how you say it
- Fighting your corner and **handling discussion effectively**

Never think of any meeting as 'their' meeting. Concentrate on your role in it and make sure you actively work at making your contribution count.

LOOKING THE PART

It was Oscar Wilde who said: 'It is only shallow people who do not judge by appearances'. How a person appears does have a tangible effect on how their words are taken. How you dress is worth a moment's thought, particularly if you are not known to everyone present.

Will you appear:

- Well prepared?
- Efficient?
- Authoritative?

- Expert?
- Well informed?
- Credible?

Everything that might contribute to how you want to be seen needs consideration. Arriving late, untidy, clutching an overflowing stack of files and spending the first few minutes rummaging through your papers in search of a particular document won't guarantee to position you as a force to be reckoned with.

If it affects how people hear your words it is important, and may need **active organisation**.

WHERE TO SIT

Does it matter where you sit? Some swear by a particular position, others do not think about it. While there will be no 'magic' seat, there are certain practicalities to be considered. For example, from a particular seat:

- Who can you see?
- Who can you not see well? (this includes the person next to you)
- What is your position with respect to the chair? Will it be easy to make yourself heard?
- Which people do you want to be able to communicate with informally? (whispering or passing a note)
- Do you want to be near or far from the telephone, coffee, door or overhead projector?
- Can you see any visual aids easily?

Some regular meetings do better if people don't always sit in the same seat, and some work well at a round table which puts no one in a commanding position at the head (think of King Arthur).

COMMUNICATE EFFECTIVELY

Never assume that communication is easy. Assume it is difficult; it is.

The quotation illustrated (attributed to various people, including ex-President Nixon) makes a good point.

Even the simplest point you want to make will need making clearly. This starts with preparation (see page 73).

Make sure you say what you mean and that you convey an accurate message.

'I know you think you understand what you think I said, but I am not sure you realise that what you heard is not what I meant'

OBEY THE RULES

Meetings would often deteriorate into a shouting match (perhaps some do anyway!) without any rules. It is in everyone's interest to obey them. This does not rule out a certain amount of assertiveness, but if you…

- Monopolise the conversation disproportionately
- Constantly interrupt others
- Become emotional or argumentative to no good purpose
- Disrupt the timetable
- Appear to be undisciplined, or worse, a troublemaker

…then you will in the long-run do your case no good. Use the chair and the agreed procedure, do not be afraid to fight your corner vigorously when appropriate, but do not lose out through what will be seen as an ill-mannered approach.

Stick to the rules – stick to the subject – and make the meeting work for you.

BREAK THE RULES!

Rules, it is said, are made to be broken. So they are. But think very carefully before you do so and do not make a habit of it – you will soon have the reputation of a troublemaker!

In any gathering some of the power and influence goes to those who are most confident, most assertive or most dramatic. There can be a time for:

- A dramatic outburst
- A fist banging on the table as 'NO' is uttered
- A display of emotion
- Some humour
- Temper (*controlled* temper)
- Interruptions

But – I repeat, but – all of this is to be used very carefully.

Make breaking the rules an exception but recognise the power of the occasional dramatic gesture.

PARTICIPATING IN THE MEETING

PREPARATION

Even the simplest meeting needs preparation. This may mean two minutes' thought or hours of careful consideration; **but it must always happen**. You will never make your point so well at meetings if you try to do so off the top of your head.

- **Read all the papers thoroughly** (past minutes, the agenda and documents or reports referred to or circulated in advance)
- **Annotate** them to highlight key points so that you can spot them fast during the meeting
- **Take note of who will be there** (what their presence might mean, who is friend and who foe, who will ask what etc)
- **Plan what you need to ask** (and how you will ask it)
- **Prepare your inputs** (almost as you would a presentation)
- **Make any notes that you will need to have in front of you** (and *never* assume you will remember every detail; write it down)

Preparation is the foundation to having an effective meeting. It is time well spent and you skimp it at your peril.

PREPARATION IN CONTEXT

Remember, your input cannot be prepared in isolation. You need to bear in mind that what you intend will be made more difficult because **people**…

- Do not listen to everything that is said (so you must hold their attention)

- Are influenced by their current views, prejudices and the status quo

- See everything from their own point of view and may find it hard to be objective

…and may misunderstand the objectives, your intentions, or take an emotive or hierarchical view of the issues involved.

PREPARATION IN CONTEXT

Events may make difficulties also. For example:

- Time may be at a premium (it is no good preparing a half hour input if you are sure to get only ten minutes)
- Other issues may take the focus off what you see as important
- It may not be possible to progress an item very far without some back-up information being available (eg costings); to try to take it on without this is not possible

Always be realistic in planning what you want to do. If you plan for the meeting that will actually happen, rather than some unlikely but ideal situation, you will do better on the day.

DO NOT BE NERVOUS

Meetings can be traumatic. There is often a great deal hanging on them and you may be conscious that the room is full of people more senior, more experienced and more expert than you.

The best antidote for nerves is **preparation**. If you have done your homework, checked your facts and thought through how to make your contribution this should give you confidence. Beyond that...

- Take a deep breath
- Ensure you have a glass of water (a dry mouth goes with butterflies in the tummy)

...and remember that the majority want – and expect – you to do perfectly well.

Some stage fright is inevitable on the big occasion. Indeed, without it the adrenalin would not flow. But, experience is soon gained, especially if you assess your performance afterwards and learn from what has happened.

Note: if your input to a meeting is 'on your feet', more in the nature of a formal presentation, then this demands additional skills. (See *The Presentations Pocketbook*).

THE SHAPE OF DISCUSSION

The way in which any item is handled during a meeting tends to follow a pattern, initially introduced by the leader. You can use this, on a smaller scale, to put over your points.

The sequence involved is:

- **Introduction** – stating the reason for the item; setting the scene; referring back to previous discussion; giving the item its own agenda: 'How I suggest we go through this is to .....'
- **Setting out the issues** – points for and against, key points (eg purpose, costs, methods, results); putting both the main issues and any other implications (political, motivational, emotive)
- **Debate** – others will now contribute; this stage should develop logical arguments and put up a picture that allows subsequent decisions to be well made
- **Summary** – with a link to further action or decision

If the stage which matters have reached is clear and each contribution falls obviously into place, the whole meeting will proceed more logically and constructively.

GET YOUR FACTS RIGHT

It is amazing how much time is spent in meetings querying, checking or challenging facts. If information proves incorrect, then a whole case can collapse or, at the very least, some credibility is lost.

Take time to check, and check again. Make sure what you say is factual. Information given out should be:

- **Explicit:** stated plainly, without being obscured by irrelevancies
- **Accurate:** exactly right
- **Precise:** just the right piece of information to make the point well

This may sound pedantic, but it matters. If you say something like: 'Change is essential. The current method is wasting 10% of the cost', and someone immediately says: 'I looked at the figures this morning and it is only 9.2%', then at once what you said is devalued. It is too late to say you only meant *about* 10%. It looks as if you did not know or were trying to overstate the case.

Be careful to state facts – factually.

MAKING AN INPUT

There are three clear objectives for what you say. It should be...

- **Understandable**   ● **Attractive**   ● **Credible**

...so that people listen, believe it is relevant and, ultimately, are prompted to agreement or action as appropriate. We will consider these in turn.

79

PARTICIPATING IN THE MEETING

MAKE WHAT YOU SAY *UNDERSTANDABLE*

You can use a number of devices to make sure what you say is understood:

- **Use clear 'signposting'**: announce what you are going to cover – 'There are three issues here; I would like to say something about costs, timing and then the problems of implementation'. If people nod to that, you can go through what becomes an agreed mini agenda and people have your comments in context

- **Use a clear structure**: even a short input needs a clear structure. Often a beginning, a middle and an end works well. Never let your comments deteriorate into a string of points prefixed only by, 'And another thing .....'

- **Follow a logical sequence**: again, signposting will make it clear. You may, for instance, opt to discuss a planned conference in terms of the chronology of the event, or a project through its major stages. Whatever the method, it must strike others as sensible and act to make the message clearer than a more random statement

MAKE WHAT YOU SAY *UNDERSTANDABLE*

- **Use visual aids**: people really do understand (and remember) more easily what they both see and hear. Consider using slides, diagrams etc – and if you have no facility for visuals, make up for it by being sufficiently descriptive; paint a picture
- **Avoid jargon**: or use it carefully. Jargon is professional slang and forms a useful shorthand for those in the know. But, never assume everyone understands the technicalities that slip off your tongue so easily
- **Avoid gobbledegook**: and 'officespeak'. Do not say: *'Considerable progress has been made in the preliminary work directed towards the establishment of the starting point and initial activities',* if you mean: 'Nothing has been done yet, but we must start soon'. Such language is trying as well as confusing

Finally, if only to remove a distraction, watch out for any irritating verbal habits such as beginning every sentence with 'Basically .....'

Understanding is the foundation – everything else you do will suffer if what you say is unclear.

MAKE WHAT YOU SAY *ATTRACTIVE*

Much that goes on at meetings is more than simply communicating information. You may have to motivate, to enthuse, to *persuade*. If you need action by others, or a particular decision made, or something implemented with commitment, it is not sufficient to *tell* people, you must *persuade* them.

This process is effectively selling. You need to:

- Identify the needs or position of other people
- Put over a case that shows them how your proposal will be acceptable or beneficial to them

If you are regularly at meetings where you need to be persuasive, then it will be worth some study. Selling and negotiation can be learned like so many other skills. (See *The Negotiator's Pocketbook*).

MAKE WHAT YOU SAY *CREDIBLE*

If you say something apparently factual which supports your case, others may at once cast doubt on it: 'You would say that, wouldn't you'.

You may well need back-up proof or evidence, such as:

- Figures and statistics
- Examples
- The collaboration of others (particularly others with clout)
- Something in writing (or, better still, published)
- Something visual or descriptive
- Something based on research
- The result of a test or trial
- Objective comment from outside the organisation
- Expert comment from an acknowledged expert

Assess whether your case needs proof from something or someone other than you, find and add such evidence to support what you propose.

DIFFERENT FORMS OF COMMUNICATION

Three key kinds of communicating take place during meetings:

- **Initiating**: proposing, suggesting and building
- **Reacting**: responding, commenting, judging, evaluating
- **Clarifying**: testing, explaining, demonstrating

Each does different things, speaks in a different 'tone' of voice and may need signposting: 'I am not asking you, I am telling you' (or vice versa).

Use them all, use them appropriately and know which is which.

DO NOT NEGLECT OBSERVATION

It is sometimes easy to get so bound up in what you are trying to do and say that you forget to observe the other participants in a meeting. Two factors are crucial here:

1. Listen

Really listen, actively listen and *take note of what is said*. Listening means adapting what you intended to say in the light of what is going on. Remember the old saying: 'People were made with one mouth, but two ears and that is a good way to use them'. You will never get your points across if they ignore what others have said.

2. Watch

Much of what we take in comes from what we see rather than hear. Watch how people respond to the meeting. Signs, gestures, expressions, body language (and non-verbal sounds such as sighs) all add to your understanding of others' position as debate continues.

Meetings demand not only that you make your point well, but that you understand the other participants – the better you do, the more accurately you can position your points.

WHEN TO SPEAK

There is no infallible rule. Open the debate and, however brilliantly you make your points, an hour later people may not really remember the points you made; leave it too late and people may have already made up their minds and be reluctant to change or prolong the discussion.

Some guidelines may help you decide what is best:

- Do not prepare on the basis of speaking at a particular stage: you need to be able to adapt what you say to fit whatever spot you finally find available

- Consider how your comments relate to others made, or anticipated, and thus when your views logically come

- Consider how you can play to your strengths. Are you best at introducing, setting out the range of things to be considered, summarising or dealing with the figures?

- When you do speak, see if you can get commitment to having a further say later: 'Perhaps I can comment again when we get to the finances involved'

Whenever you opt to have your say, never leave it too late. Perpetually waiting for the 'best' moment may end up removing your ability to get a word in at all.

PARTICIPATING IN THE MEETING

ADOPT THE RIGHT ATTITUDE

Participating in a meeting is an *active* process. Certainly, if you hope to gain anything from it you cannot go to sleep!

Remember:

- **Remain alert and concentrate throughout**
- **Listen to everything that is said** (and make notes as necessary)
- **Watch how other people appear** (part of understanding comes through body language)
- **Keep thinking** (and engage your brain before your mouth as you contribute!)
- **Remain calm** (whatever the provocation)

Keep your wits about you if you wish to make an impression.

PARTICIPATING IN THE MEETING

DEVELOP YOUR SKILLS

Meetings are complex. They are interactive, and it is difficult to predict who will do and say what. Being competent at participating in meetings is not something most of us are born with. We can all benefit from studying the various communications skills meetings require – and from practice.

If you do not have much experience of attending meetings then you need to go to some more. While being careful not to waste time, consider:

- What meetings are held
- Which committees or management groups you might join
- What your role and responsibilities enable you to contribute to particular gatherings

Get round some tables, join some groups, see how it works and experiment with your style of participation. Think about how you perform and fine-tune your skills. Remember, being effective in meetings is a highly necessary business and career skill.

GROUP DYNAMICS

GROUP DYNAMICS

WORKING TOGETHER

There is an old saying that a meeting is a gathering of people who *singly* can do nothing, but who *together* can decide that nothing can be done!

Hopefully the reverse is true. There are issues that need debate, consultation and the creative element that arises from people working constructively together.

For this to be the case participants must:

- Accept that working together can be difficult
- Work to actively remove the difficulties
- Work also to actively encourage the potential synergy
- Use the dynamics of the group to prompt the positive processes that are wanted

Make the outcome of the meeting greater than that which could be achieved individually.

SOCIAL STRUCTURE

Organisations are made up of people; they have a social structure. Contact and communication amongst people are important and cannot be cut off. An organisation that never had any meetings would be a sterile place.

Meetings must be businesslike, but time may have to be allowed for those present to…

- Meet
- Exchange information (and gossip)
- Update their experience

…and interact in a way that makes them feel part of a team, and makes that team something they want to be a part of.

Without this social interaction they may be frustrated and not find it easy to get down to business. Or they may simply not want to take part. As the columnist Katherine Whitehorn said:

'Meetings..... are rather like cocktail parties. You don't want to go, but you are cross not to be asked.'

GROUP DYNAMICS

GROUP MOTIVATION

Groups, just like teams, are internally motivated. If the group is strongly motivated to achieve its goals then it will get down to business constructively. Sometimes comments made in meetings reflect the group mentality more than any one individual's, so it is worth concentrating on factors that enhance a positive feeling within the group. Such factors include:

- Everyone understanding the purpose
- No major conflicts between individual and group intentions
- Having (and putting up with) no 'passengers'
- No dissatisfaction with, or distrust of, the chair
- Team loyalty
- Experience of working successfully together
- No destructive cliques
- Confidence in their joint and individual abilities
- No hierarchical hang-ups

A well motivated group always works together better than a disparate one in which morale is low.

HOW MUCH DISCUSSION?

Meetings can veer from monologue to free for all. The amount of discussion, debate and the freedom with which it is allowed to roam far and wide will influence the way the meeting proceeds.

Too much discussion, poorly controlled, may produce:

- Too many alternatives or details to handle at one time
- Too much emotion
- More frequent misunderstandings
- Opposing sides emerging
- More time taken to reach conclusion or no conclusion at all
- Digression into minor issues
- Lack of attention to necessary detail
- Circular arguments
- Drift into a lack of realism

HOW MUCH DISCUSSION?

Restricted debate, too tightly controlled, may produce:

- Boredom
- Undue attention to detail – 'nitpicking'
- Repetition
- Withholding of key information
- Over hasty decisions
- Disorganised follow-up action
- No real commitment to decisions taken
- Decisions not supported later
- Unbreakable disagreement
- Low morale and lack of enthusiasm
- Fixation with past

AFTER THE MEETING

THE MINUTES

Are they necessary? For some meetings the answer is, 'NO'. There is more than enough paperwork in most organisations already.

On some occasions minutes will be necessary; more often, **some sort of simple 'action reminder' will be essential**. A written note after the meeting serves three specific purposes:

- A **prompt to action**, a reminder to those who have taken on tasks at the meeting to do them and do them on time

- An **aide memoire at the next meeting**, forming a link between sessions of regular meetings, ensuring that points are reported or progressed further. This is often represented on the agenda as 'matters arising'

- A **record** of what has occurred and, particularly, what decisions have been made. This may be an essential permanent record or merely a convenience over a month or two, depending on the nature of the meeting

Only prepare minutes when it is really necessary; but think very carefully before you entirely omit any sort of written note.

MINUTES: MAKE THEM USEFUL

If notes are to be useful and effective they must be:

- **Accurate:** this is obvious but important; any sloppiness of reporting or omissions can cause problems
- **Objective:** whoever prepares them must report what was said, not inject their particular view
- **Succinct:** unless they summarise effectively they are likely to go unread
- **Understandable:** if they are to provide a useful spur to action and a correct record they must be clear
- **Businesslike:** making it clear *what* action is expected of *whom*, by *when*. Many organisations will have their own standard of layout and presentation

Notes are a waste if no one looks at them; but they must earn a reading.

MINUTES: A PRACTICAL LAYOUT

Notes should follow a planned set of headings:

Those present: this may be important to the record (as may be who they are, eg someone acting as a representative of a department or staff association).

Apologies: it may later be useful to know whose input was not available.

Minutes of the last meeting: if the meeting is one of a series this item may produce comment that needs recording.

Matters arising: in numbered paragraphs as necessary.

Items discussed: in numbered paragraphs that report the facts and the decisions (sometimes with detail of the discussion). Usually a 'reported' style ('It was agreed that .....') is best, avoiding any tendency for the record to veer towards what the reporter feels *might* or *should* have happened.

Other headings can be added as necessary, such as **Any other business** or **Date of the next meeting**.

Finally, consider and, if necessary, list everyone who needs a copy (often more than those who attended or sent apologies) and circulate the information promptly.

MINUTES: BEST FORMAT

Notes, and especially more formal minutes, should not be set out as solid pages of dense type. People may wish to annotate them, so give them plenty of space.

The key elements that should jump out from the style and layout are:

- Decisions
- Actions
- Who will take action
- The form of that action
- The date by which it will be completed

For example:

ITEM	ACTION	DATE
It was decided that a breakdown of the costs involved in the project would be prepared and circulated before the next meeting.	P.F. to prepare 1 page summary	Circulate by 15 Dec

AFTER THE MEETING

MINUTES: ISSUE IMMEDIATELY

A final piece of advice: if you are responsible for compiling the minutes then **do so as soon as possible after the meeting has ended**.

- You are simply much more likely to remember the detail accurately (because of this they should also take less time to prepare)

- Many people will not get down to the action they may have promised until the minutes arrive, so early circulation can reduce delay in implementation

- Prompt action appears efficient which may set an appropriate example or position you in the right light

Moral: resist putting off what can be seen as a chore; it can pay dividends.

MEETINGS PROCEDURE

For the more formal meetings only

MEETINGS PROCEDURE

RULES OF PROCEDURE

The best guideline here is to have as few rules as the circumstances allow – no one wants to spend excessive time on red tape. (The exception may be an association with a formal constitution, where more elaborate rules are essential).

Sensible rules in certain areas, however, may keep matters on track, save time and help achieve better results. For example, you might specify:

- Length of notice necessary to call a meeting (and who can initiate it)
- Where and when it is acceptable to hold it (meetings have been called for a Sunday and scheduled miles from participants to discourage attendance)
- Agendas and reports to be tabled: form and style, when they should be prepared and circulated
- The role of the chair (obeying rules, making comments only via the chair etc)
- Language: no raised voices or bad language
- Declaring individual interests

Do watch out for any legal implications resulting (eg on staff matters).

 Whatever rules you have, make sure they are sensible, agreed and known to all.

MEETINGS PROCEDURE

SPECIFIC RULES

Where formalities are essential, the key factors – any of which might, on occasion, be important to meetings happening regularly within typical organisations – are:

Quorums

At some meetings important decisions cannot be made without a representative number of those involved; a committee may only be able to progress matters with, say, 50% of its members present. Some rules may need to be laid down here (without any there is opportunity for deviousness).

Motions

This is simply a form of words intended to stand on the record, used:

- To start a discussion
- After discussion to summarise and agree action

Motions may need to be tabled in advance, proposed and seconded formally, dealt with before the meeting moves on and voted on. The way in which this is to work in a particular meeting must be clear to all concerned. Note: particular care is needed in the wording of motions; this must be clear, positive and unambiguous.

MEETINGS PROCEDURE

SPECIFIC RULES

Amendments

These add to or subtract from a motion or change it in some way. Formal meetings may need amendments proposing and seconding. There are two types:

- Constructive (adding to the case; acceptable to the proposer of the original motion)
- 'Wrecking' (designed to change the whole basis of discussion)

Either must be dealt with before the original motion can be adopted or rejected.

Voting

Whether this involves a simple show of hands or something more formal (eg a paper – and confidential – vote) the procedure, and the result, should be absolutely clear, agreed and recorded so that it is never a matter of disagreement or argument.

Points of order/information

These are interjections to the formal proceedings of the meeting, the first to indicate a breach of agreed rules (point of order), the second to correct something that has been said and is *factually* incorrect.

 To remain useful such formalities should be kept solely as a means to an end. They should never become an end in themselves.

SUMMARY

CHECKLIST

At the end of any meeting you should review its effectiveness; only in this way can future meetings be improved. The following sets out the sort of questions to ask:

The objectives for the meeting
- Were there clear and valid reasons to meet?
- Were these reasons spelt out in terms of measurable objectives?
- Did participants know these objectives in advance, and agree with them (were there other, more personal, things people hoped to come from the meeting)?

Administration
- Was sufficient notice given?
- Was sufficient and clear information given (agenda, relevant papers, previous minutes etc)?
- Were the location, environment and equipment organised and appropriate?

The people
- Were the right people in attendance? (In particular, were there people there unnecessarily or were key players missing?)

CHECKLIST

Inputs
- Were formal inputs prepared?
- Did people put over their cases clearly and succinctly?
- Were inputs backed by appropriate documentation where necessary?
- Did people stick to the point?

Interaction
- Were those making formal inputs able to answer supplementary questions well?
- Did everyone participate, as required?
- Did people listen?
- Did they follow the rules and proceed in an orderly fashion?
- Were discussions constructive and directed towards the objectives?
- Had everyone done any necessary homework?
- Were there disruptions (caused by, for instance, emotion, the taking of a parochial view, or sheer bloody-mindedness)?

SUMMARY

CHECKLIST

The chair/leader
- Were the meeting and the people appropriately introduced?
- Was the agenda used, and adhered to?
- Was time well managed? (Did the meeting start and finish on time; was the right amount of time spent on each item?)
- Were the people well managed – brought into the discussion (or shut up!) as appropriate?
- Did the chair remain impartial?
- Was the discussion regularly summarised?
- Was order maintained?
- Were any necessary formalities observed?
- Overall was the meeting directed in a way that prompted it to deal with the right matters, in the right way and draw real conclusions and make planned decisions?

Given clear objectives, any meeting must be judged on whether it achieved them or not; and, in the long-term, on the quality of the decisions and action flowing from the time and deliberations it entailed.

SUMMARY

FURTHER READING

Meetings involve a variety of overlapping skills, such as communication in all its forms, and also powers of persuasion and negotiation. Several other pocketbooks provide relevant information including these two, both of which are written by Patrick Forsyth:

- *The Sales Excellence Pocketbook:* primarily for those in sales, but offers useful thoughts on being persuasive

- *The Negotiator's Pocketbook:* has relevance for many situations encountered in meetings

Two other short books by Patrick Forsyth, which may be useful are:

30 Minutes to get your own way and *30 Minutes before your Presentation* (Kogan Page) which look at effective and persuasive communication and at formal presentation.

Whatever you do, remember that performing well in meetings is a key to success both for your role in your organisation, and for your career in business; if some further study will assist you to achieve the standard you want, the results will justify the effort.

FINALLY...

We will return at the end to something mentioned earlier, that ubiquitous agenda item: A. O. B. (Any Other Business). So often this comes at the end of the meeting. There is a sigh of relief, the end is in sight: 'Just a few A.O.B. items' says the chairperson ..... and the meeting nosedives into another half hour of inconsequential bits and pieces, often gripes, admin and irrelevances. People leave irritated and the impact of a good meeting is lost.

Good meetings start with A.O.B. Good chairpeople give 10 minutes, or whatever, to this, get the dregs, as it were, out of the way and then ...

... end with a bang!

...making sure they send people away on the note, a high note, *they* want!

About the Author

Patrick Forsyth
Patrick runs Touchstone Training and
Consultancy, an independent firm specialising
in work in marketing, sales and management and
communication skills. With more than twenty years
experience as a consultant, he has worked with clients in a
wide range of industries and in many different parts of the
world. He also conducts courses for a number of
management institutes.

He is the author of five other pocketbooks and a number of
other successful business books including: *How to write
Reports and Proposals, Successful Time Management, How
to craft successful Business Presentations* and *Detox your
Career*. He has books in 22 languages and writes regularly
for a number of business journals.

Contact
Patrick can be contacted at:
Touchstone Training & Consultancy, 28 Saltcote Maltings,
Heybridge, Maldon, Essex CM9 4QP, UK
Tel/Fax: + 44 (0) 1621 859300
Email: Patrick@touchstonetc.freeserve.co.uk

MANAGEMENT POCKETBOOKS

Published by:
Management Pocketbooks Ltd,
Laurel House, Station Approach,
Alresford, Hants S024 9JH UK

© Patrick Forsyth 1994 and 2004.
All rights reserved.

First edition published 1994 and
reprinted 1997, 1998, 1999, 2001
and 2003. This edition published
2004. Reprinted 2005, 2007.

ISBN: 978 1 903776 278

Design, typesetting and graphics
by **efex ltd**.   Printed in UK

British Library Cataloguing-in-
Publication Data – a catalogue
record for this book is available
from the British Library.

ORDER FORM

Your details

Name _____

Position _____

Company _____

Address _____

_____

Telephone _____

Fax _____

E-mail _____

VAT No. (EC companies) _____

Your Order Ref _____

Please send me:

	No. copies
The Meetings Pocketbook	
The _____ Pocketbook	
The _____ Pocketbook	
The _____ Pocketbook	
The _____ Pocketbook	

Order by Post
MANAGEMENT POCKETBOOKS LTD
LAUREL HOUSE, STATION APPROACH,
ALRESFORD, HAMPSHIRE SO24 9JH UK
Order by Phone, Fax or Internet
Telephone: +44 (0)1962 735573
Facsimile: +44 (0)1962 733637
E-mail: sales@pocketbook.co.uk
Web: www.pocketbook.co.uk

MANAGEMENT POCKETBOOKS